Magnificent Mazes
20th Century

Anna Nilsen

How to Play
Find out through
the time tunnel.

TIME TUNNEL

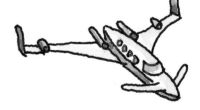
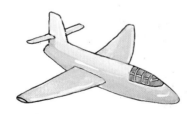

3

Sometimes you will have to go backwards as well as forwards.

4

Jump through time tunnels. DO NOT CROSS THEM.

6

You can go across landing pads.

8

The ending place will be labelled like this.

Marie Curie ends here

7

You will know you have reached the correct time zone when you see your chosen character and their destination spot here at the bottom of the page.

Marie Curie ends here

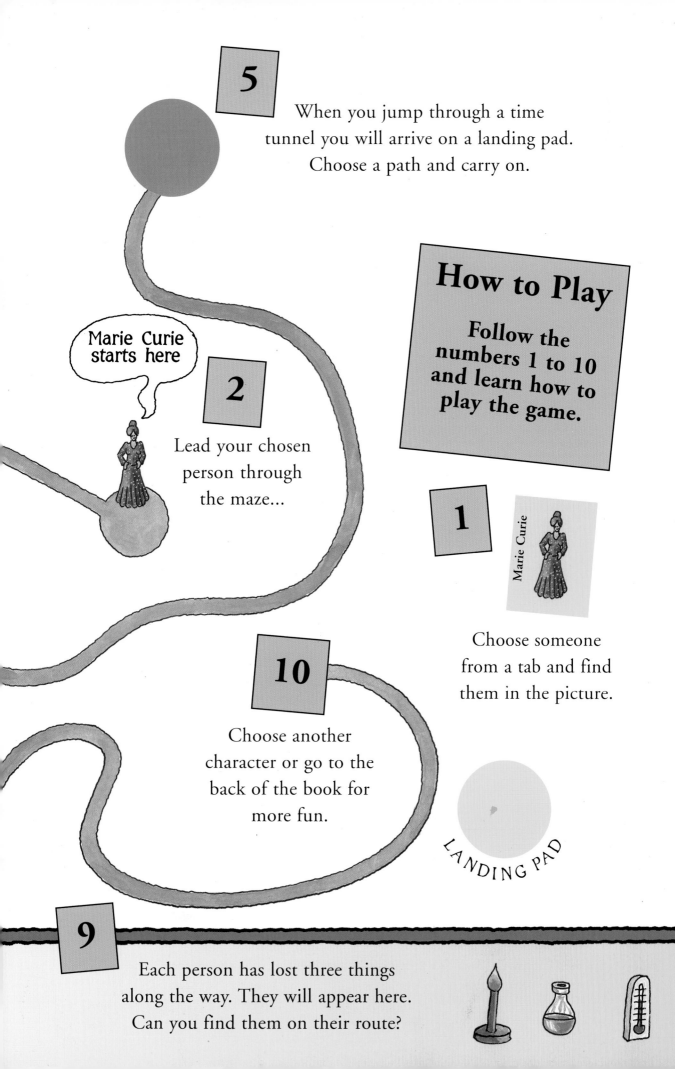

5

When you jump through a time tunnel you will arrive on a landing pad. Choose a path and carry on.

Marie Curie starts here

2

Lead your chosen person through the maze...

How to Play

Follow the numbers 1 to 10 and learn how to play the game.

1

Marie Curie

Choose someone from a tab and find them in the picture.

10

Choose another character or go to the back of the book for more fun.

LANDING PAD

9

Each person has lost three things along the way. They will appear here. Can you find them on their route?

 Marie Curie
at her lab in Paris, France 1911.

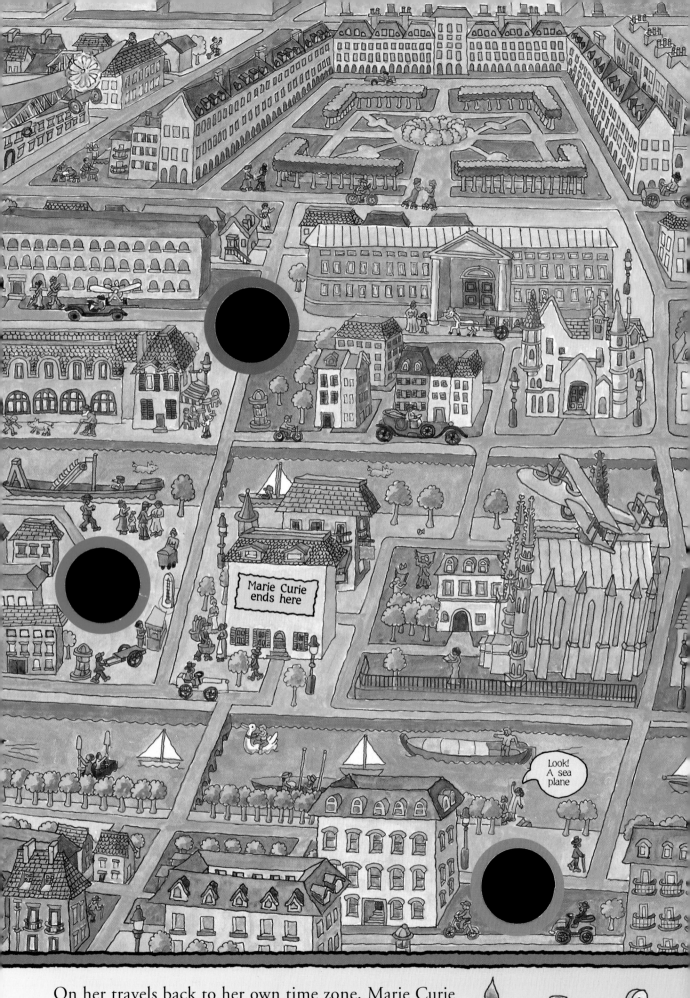

On her travels back to her own time zone, Marie Curie
lost these three things. Can you find them?

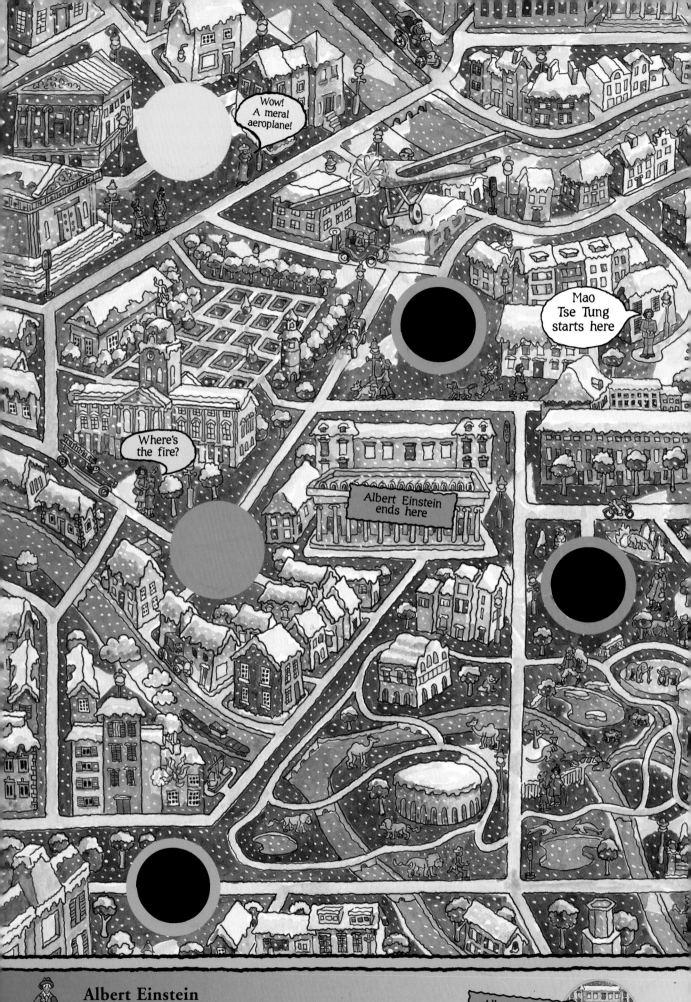

Albert Einstein

at Berlin University, Germany 1923.

On his travels back to his own time zone, Albert Einstein lost these three things. Can you find them?

 Pablo Picasso
at Chateau Vauvenargues Arles, France 1938.

Pablo Picasso
ends here

Love all!

Pelé

On his travels back to his own time zone, Pablo Picasso
lost these three things. Can you find them?

Mahatma Gandhi
in Bombay, India 1946.

On his travels back to his own time zone, Mahatma Gandhi lost these three things. Can you find them?

 Marilyn Monroe

in her first film in Hollywood, U.S.A. 1952.

On her travels back to her own time zone, Marilyn Monroe lost these three things. Can you find them?

Penalty kick!

Pelé ends here

Pelé

a football star in Rio de Janiero, Brazil 1958.

Pelé ends here

On his travels back to his own time zone, Pelé lost these three things. Can you find them?

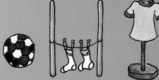

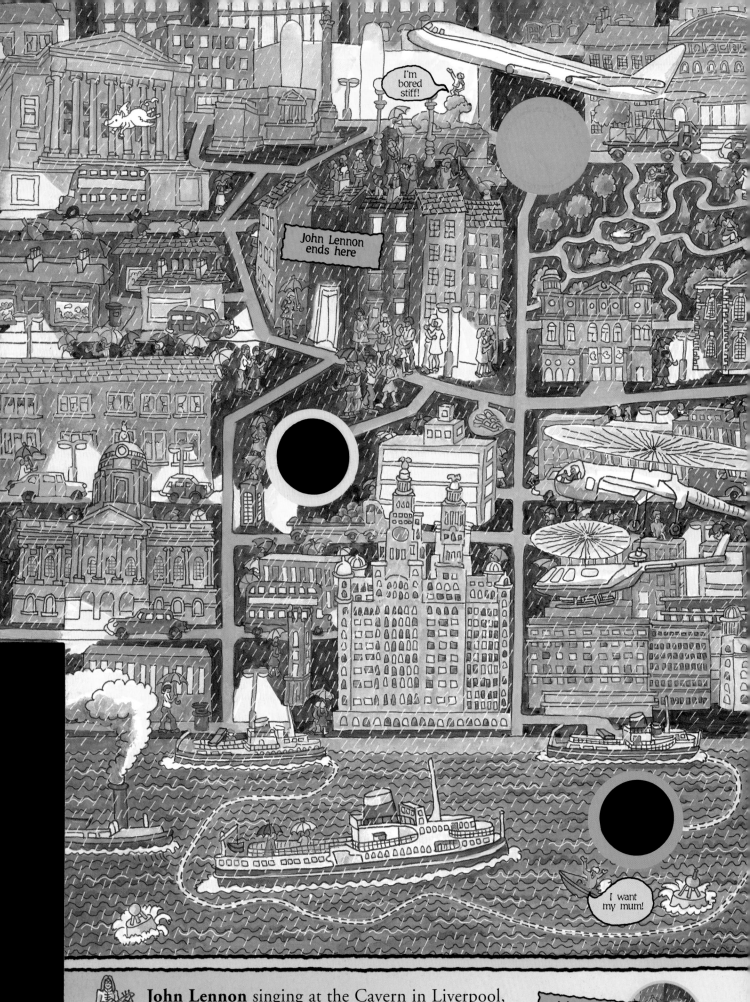

 John Lennon singing at the Cavern in Liverpool, United Kingdom 1961.

John Lennon ends here

On his travels back to his own time zone, John Lennon
lost these three things. Can you find them?

Mao Tse Tung

declares a Cultural Revolution in Peking, China 1974.

On his travels back to his own time zone, Mao Tse Tung lost these three things. Can you find them?

There's the jail!

 Nelson Mandela freed from jail near Cape Town, South Africa 1990.

 Nelson Mandela ends here

On his travels back to his own time zone, Nelson Mandela lost these three things. Can you find them?

Bill Gates

in his cyber space, Redmond, U.S.A. 1999.

On his travels back to his own time zone, Bill Gates lost these three things. Can you find them?

Marie Curie
Paris
1911

Picasso
Arles
1938

Marilyn Monroe
Hollywood
1952

Einstein
Berlin
1923

Gandhi
Bombay
1946

1900

1950

Telescope Game

How much did you really
see on the maze routes?
Look at these views
and work out where they
came from.

Notre Dame
is a fine medieval
Cathedral.

The Cavern was the
club where the Beatles
first played in 1961.

Muslims pray in the
direction of the Ka'ba, the
first place of worship.

The Brandenberg Gate
was one of 18 gates in
the city wall.

The Berlin Wall
was dismantled
in 1989.

The Maracana Stadium
hosted the 1958
World Cup Final.

Suffragettes demanded
rights for women
and the vote.

Nelson Mandela was
imprisoned in the
jail on Robben Island.

The popular French
game *Boules* was first
played in 1910.

Mont St Victoire
was famously painted
by Cézanne.

Niagra Falls was
Marilyn Monroe's
first film.

The Great Wall is the
biggest fortification ever built
in the world.

Blériot was the
first man to fly the
channel in 1909.

Count Ferdinand von
Zeppelin designed many
spectacular airships.

Alcock and Brown were the first people to fly over the Atlantic Ocean in 1919.

The world famous Rio Carnival is held 40 days before Lent.

To Hindu people the cow is a sacred animal.

Silent movies were often accompanied by live music.

The Hall of Prayer for Good Harvests, lies in the Temple of Heaven.

The stealth bomber, developed in 1981, is invisible on radar screens.

This convertible Renault was the first left-hand drive car.

The Royal Liver Building was the first reinforced concrete building.

The lettering at Hollywood was built in 1923 15m high.

This mausoleum honours the life of the great leader Mao Tse Tung.

The Berlin Zoo is the ninth oldest zoo in the world.

Special baskets were designed to carry long baguettes loaves.

These boats were immortalised in the song *Ferry 'Cross the Mersey.*

This huge statue of Christ the Redeemer looks out over Rio.

The Gateway of India commemorates King George V's visit in 1911.

Crowds welcomed Mandela when freed from jail in 1990.

Who they
were and when
they lived.

Paris, France 1911

Marie Curie was a Polish scientist. She and her husband Pierre discovered radium in 1903 whilst working in their lab in Paris. They were awarded the Nobel Prize for Physics that year and in 1911 Marie was awarded the Nobel Prize for Chemistry.

Marie Curie
(1867 - 1934)

Berlin, Germany 1923

German physicist Albert Einstein was most famous for his "theory of relativity" which advanced the development of nuclear science. He won the Nobel Prize for Physics in 1921. He later moved from Switzerland to live in America.

Albert Einstein
(1879 -1955)

Arles, France 1938

Pablo Picasso was one of the most prolific, versatile and inventive artists of the twentieth century. Born in Spain, he later lived and worked in Paris. In his lifetime he worked in and developed a variety of artistic styles, including his "blue period" and cubism.

Pablo Picasso
(1881 - 1973)

Bombay, India 1946

Gandhi studied law in England but later returned to India to become the leader of the Indian National Congress. He supported the cause of Indian independence and was imprisoned for his attempts to banish the British. He was eventually assassinated after conflict erupted between the Hindus and Muslims.

Mahatma Gandhi
(1869 - 1948)

Hollywood, U.S.A. 1952

Marilyn Monroe was a model and media celebrity and appeared in her first film, *Niagra*, in1952. She went on to star in many other films, the most famous of which is probably *Some Like it Hot*. She was married three times and committed suicide at the age of thirty-six.

Marilyn Monroe
(1926 -1962)